鲁比·布里奇斯

Heroes and Role Models | Non-Fiction Series

Copyright © 2022 by Level Learning, INC. and Washington Yu Ying PCS™
Original and Edited Text Copyright © 2022 by Washington Yu Ying PCS™

All rights reserved. No part of this book in whole or part may be reproduced without written permission from the publisher.

Published by Level Learning, INC.

Content Contributors:
Washington Yu Ying PCS™
Level Learning - Ya-Ching Chang

Illustrations by: Josh Taira

Leveling classification based on Level Learning standard. For full description, visit www.levellearning.com

ISBN 978-1-64040-009-2
Simplified Chinese Edition

About Level Learning:
Level Learning provides a literacy focused curriculum specifically designed for K-12 Chinese as a Second Language classrooms. Our program offers 20 levels of specific and detailed objectives, leveled texts and passages, mastery-based online assessment, and analytics to enable data-driven instruction. Level Learning reading curriculum for both literature and informational text emphasize grammar and comprehension skills to help teachers develop confident and independent Chinese language readers. The non-fiction series of books are specifically designed to support our informational text course based on multiple national standards. To learn more about our entire offering, visit www.levellearning.com.

About Washington Yu Ying PCS™:
Washington Yu Ying PCS is a Mandarin English dual language immersion International Baccalaureate (IB) World school. Yu Ying's mission is to inspire and prepare young people to create a better world by challenging them to reach their full potential in a nurturing Chinese/English educational environment. Yu Ying's comprehensive IB, dual immersion curriculum equips students with global competencies for success in the real world. As a leader in immersion education, Yu Ying is determined to advance Chinese language programs and global citizenry education by helping other schools create and strengthen their Chinese programs. For more information, email: products@washingtonyuying.org

在1950年到1970年期间，许多美国人觉得白人和非洲裔是不一样的。白人和非洲裔在不同的学校读书；在不同的餐馆吃饭；在不同的地方居住。这种现象被称为"种族隔离"。

当时的美国政府想做一些改变。政府想让白人和非洲裔生活在同样的环境里。但是，住在美国南方的许多白人并不喜欢这个改变。

在1960年,有一个叫鲁比的非洲裔女孩到白人的学校上学。这件事受到许多人的反对,因为人们不希望非洲裔出现在白人的学校里。许多父母也不希望他们的孩子和非洲裔一起上学。

鲁比上学的第一天,有一群人聚集在学校外面抗议。这些人不停地喊叫着,叫鲁比赶快离开这所学校。为了保护鲁比,警察只好陪着她一起进入学校。但是鲁比一点也不害怕,因为她相信这是一所很好的学校。

进入学校后,鲁比却被叫到校长室,因为有许多老师和学生不想和鲁比一起上课。后来,终于有一位老师愿意给鲁比上课了。虽然教室里只有她和老师两个人,鲁比还是很认真地听课。

刚开始去学校的这几天，鲁比知道自己不受欢迎，但是她还是鼓起勇气去学校。就这样一天又一天，鲁比每天都去上学。第二年，鲁比慢慢地交到了一些朋友，其他人也愿意和她一起上课了。老师和学生慢慢地看到鲁比和大家一样的地方，而不再只关注她的肤色了。

后来，越来越多的人知道了鲁比的故事。有人把她的故事拍成影片，也有人把她的故事写成书。现在，大家相信"种族融合"，而不再是"种族隔离"了。现在，不只是白人和非洲裔，其他很多不同种族、不同肤色的人也都平等地生活在一起了。

Glossary

	Pinyin	English Definition
非洲裔	fēi zhōu yì	African descent
一样	yí yàng	same
餐馆	cān guǎn	restaurant
居住	jū zhù	to live
现象	xiàn xiàng	phenomenon
种族隔离	zhǒng zú gé lí	racial segregation
政府	zhèng fǔ	government
改变	gǎi biàn	change
同样	tóng yàng	the same
环境	huán jìng	surrounding
受到	shòu dào	receive
反对	fǎn duì	against, disagreement
出现	chū xiàn	to appear
上学	shàng xué	to go to school
聚集	jù jí	to gather

	Pinyin	English Definition
抗议	kàng yì	to protest
喊叫	hǎn jiào	to yell, to scream
赶快	gǎn kuài	hurry up
离开	lí kāi	to leave
保护	bǎo hù	to protect
陪	péi	to accompany
害怕	hài pà	afraid
相信	xiāng xìn	to believe
校长室	xiào zhǎng shì	Principal's office
愿意	yuàn yì	willing
教室	jiào shì	classroom
认真	rèn zhēn	serious
欢迎	huān yíng	welcome
鼓起	gǔ qǐ	to muster
勇气	yǒng qì	courage

	Pinyin	English Definition
关注	guān zhù	to pay attention
肤色	fū sè	skin color
越来越多	yuè lái yuè duō	more and more
影片	yǐng piān	movie
种族融合	zhǒng zú róng hé	racial integration

www.ingramcontent.com/pod-product-compliance
Lightning Source LLC
Chambersburg PA
CBHW041225070526
44584CB00001B/100